DATE DUE

GROUNDBREAKERS

Dian Fossey

Richard and Sara Wood

Heinemann Library
Chicago, Illinois

Designed by Tessa Barwick
Printed in Hong Kong

05 04 03 02 01
10 9 8 7 6 5 4 3 2

Library of Congress Cataloging-in-Publication Data
Wood, Richard, 1949 May 6-
    Dian Fossey / Richard Wood, Sara Wood.
        p. cm -- (Groundbreakers)
    Includes bibliographical references (p.).
    ISBN 1-58810-049-9
    1. Fossey, Dian--Juvenile literature. 2. Primatologists--United States--Biography. [1. Fossey, Dian. 2. Zoologists. 3. Women--Biography. 4. Gorilla.] I. Wood, Sara, 1952- II. Title. III. Series.

    QL31.F65 W66 2001
    599.884'092--dc21
    [B]
                                    00-059683

Acknowledgments
The publishers would like to thank the following for permission to reproduce photographs: Bruce Coleman Collection , p. 30; Bruce Coleman Collection/ Werner Layer, p. 43; Corbis/Staffan Widstrand, p. 12; Corbis/Hulton-Deutsch, p. 13; Corbis/Jonathan Blair, p. 14; Corbis/Robert Maass, p. 15; Corbis/Karl Ammann, p. 39; Dian Fossey Gorilla Fund, Europe, p. 16; Bob Campbell, pp. 18, 22, 23, 24, 25, 31, 33; Ian Redmond,, pp. 21, 26, 27, 28, 29, 34, 35, 36, 38, 40, 41; Kosair Children's Hospital, p. 7; MPM Images, p. 4; Oxford Scientific Films, p. 9; Oxford Scientific Films/Joan Root, p. 10; Oxford Scientific Films//Michael Leach, p. 19; Andrew Plumptre/Peter Newark's American Pictures, p. 6; Rex Features, p. 5; Veit-Watkins/SIPA, pp. 11, 17, 37; 1988 Images, p. 42; Still Pictures , p. 11; Frans Lanting, p. 32.

Cover photograph reproduced with the permission of Dian Fossey Gorilla Fund, Europe/Ian Redmond.

Some words are shown in bold, **like this.** You can find out what they mean by looking in the glossary.

Contents

The country called Zaire in the text has had many different names. When Dian first went to Africa, in 1963, it was called The Republic of the Congo. In 1966 the name changed to the Democratic Republic of the Congo. From 1971 until 1997 it was called Zaire, but now it is called the Democratic Republic of the Congo. In this book it is called Zaire, because that is what Dian Fossey called it.

The Gorillas' Champion

Mention Dian Fossey, and most people immediately think of Africa and gorillas. But Fossey's own origins could hardly have been more different from the tropical rain forests of Rwanda. She was born in 1932 in Fairfax, California. Fairfax was a comfortable, middle-class suburb of San Francisco, a prosperous city. It was about as far removed as you can get from the Africa Dian would come to know so well.

Dian grew up in San Francisco, California. She never liked city life, and longed to escape to work in the countryside.

In Fossey's words:

"Neither destiny nor fate took me to Africa. Nor was it romance. I had a deep wish to see and live with wild animals in a world that hadn't yet been completely changed by humans. I guess I really wanted to go backward in time."

(From a quotation in *Woman in the Mists,* by Farley Mowat, 1987)

So what took this seemingly typical American girl away from her safe surroundings into a world of great discomfort and danger—and, ultimately, to a violent death? It was certainly not her parents. They hoped that Dian would study business and settle down near home. Nor was it her early schooling. As a young student she was, in fact, far from successful. Fossey loved animals and wanted to be a veterinarian, but she failed the entrance exams, and could not get in to veterinary school.

A closer look

Perhaps it was these early failures that made Dian so determined to prove herself. She never learned how to compromise. Her single-minded attitude often got her into trouble, but it was also what drove her on to success. By the time of her death in 1985, Dian Fossey was one of the best-known **conservationists** of the twentieth century.

Fossey's contribution to science was to develop new ways of observing **primates,** and recording their behavior, at close range. Her legacy to the world at large is that she saved the mountain gorilla from almost certain **extinction.** Thanks to Dian Fossey, there are more wild mountain gorillas alive today than when she first went to Africa in 1963. She certainly helped to change our view of gorillas from savage monsters to gentle giants.

Dian Fossey always felt more at home with her animal friends than she did with people.

ONGOING IMPACT   New insight

Dian Fossey had none of the education and training normally required for the scientific study of animals. But despite this—or perhaps because of it—she was able to develop new methods of study, such as close observation and imitating the behavior of animals, that have helped field researchers ever since.

Dian's Early Years

The economic depression of the 1930s affected many Americans, like these men lining up for food at a soup kitchen. Dian's father lost his job and left home.

Dian Fossey did not have a happy childhood. As a small child, she admired her glamorous mother, who worked as a fashion model, but felt closer to her father. Unfortunately, his business prospects as an insurance salesman suffered from the worldwide **economic depression** of the 1930s. As he struggled to pay the family bills, he increasingly turned to alcohol. When Dian was six years old, her parents divorced. Within a year, her mother had remarried. Dian's new stepfather, Richard Price, was a successful builder. But as a parent, he was distant, cold, and strict. Until she was ten years old, Dian was made to eat her meals in the kitchen with the housekeeper.

Dian was not a healthy child. She suffered from **asthma** and had regular bouts of **pneumonia.** She was not allowed any pets except one goldfish. However, she loved animals and was able to form close bonds with many of them, from a horse to a friend's pet coyote. She took riding lessons, joined a riding club, and spent one summer vacation working on a ranch in Montana.

By the time she was fourteen years old, Dian was over six feet tall and embarrassed about her height. She towered over her mother, who was so concerned that she took Dian to the doctor to see if anything could be done about it. Dian thought of herself as plain, even ugly. She became painfully shy. She seemed to feel more relaxed with animals than with other people.

Changing course

When Dian left Lowell High School in 1948, her stepfather persuaded her to take a business studies course at a local junior college. She hated it. After two years, she switched to a **preveterinary** course at the University of California, hoping at last to fulfill her dream of working with animals. But it was not to be. Although she excelled in **zoology** and biology, she failed physics and chemistry. Reluctantly, she changed courses again, this time to **occupational therapy.**

Once she earned her degree, Dian was at last able to escape from California—and from her family. She found work at Kosair Children's Hospital in Louisville, Kentucky, as director of occupational therapy. Although Dian found that she had a natural talent for working with the children there, it was not what she really wanted to do. She made her home in a run-down farm cottage surrounded by animals—farm dogs, cattle, and the raccoons and opossums that lived there. She still longed to work with animals.

This is part of Kosair Children's Hospital in Louisville, Kentucky, as it looks today. The picture shows the building in which Dian worked.

People who knew Dian often said that she preferred animals to humans and had few close friends. However, she did become close to the Henrys, a well-known Louisville family, through their daughter, Mary, a friend from Kosair Hospital. When Mary returned from an African safari, Dian listened enviously to her tales of adventure in the bush. Mary also introduced her to Pookie Forrester, a handsome young farmer from Rhodesia, the country now called Zimbabwe, who was visiting the United States. Dian dreamed of visiting him in Africa. Unfortunately, the cost of such a trip was too high for her to manage on her small salary. Dian's parents refused to lend her the money, saying the trip was "madness." But Dian's determination knew no limits. She took out a bank loan to pay for the trip and, in September 1963, flew off for a seven-week tour of central Africa.

Meeting Dr. Leakey

Dian was no ordinary tourist. She did not follow the standard, safe safari routes. Instead, she hired a specialist guide to take her into remote regions in search of wildlife. In Tanzania, she first met Dr. Louis Leakey, the famous **anthropologist.**

The Virunga Volcanoes of central Africa are home to the mountain gorilla.

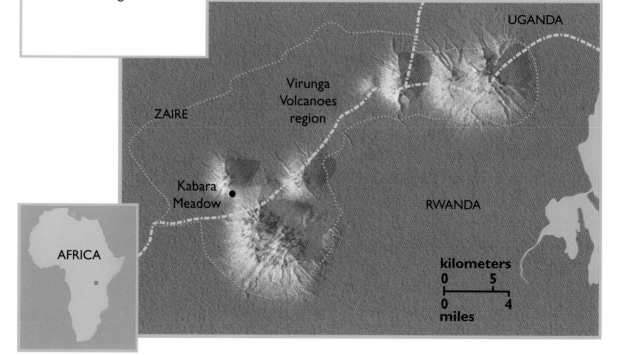

UGANDA

Virunga
Volcanoes
region

ZAIRE

Kabara
Meadow

RWANDA

AFRICA

kilometers
0   5

0   4
miles

Dian slipped and injured her ankle while climbing into a gorge, and it was so painful that she got sick over some fossils that Leakey was digging up. Their meeting was an important turning point for Dian. When Leakey mentioned the endangered gorillas of the Virunga mountain region, Dian decided to see them for herself.

Love at first sight

Dian arrived at Mount Mikeno in the Congo two weeks later. She was clearly a very determined woman, since the thin air aggravated her **asthma,** her ankle was still sore, and her face was swollen by allergies and fever. After a difficult climb of almost seven hours, she reached Kabara Meadow, an established gorilla-watching base. There, she met up with the wildlife photographers Alan and Joan Root. They reluctantly agreed to let her accompany Sanwekwe, their **tracker,** into the forest in search of gorillas. For two days, Dian and Sanwekwe saw nothing. But on the third day, they suddenly heard a loud *"wraagh"* close by. Sanwekwe cut an opening in the bush with his ***panga* knife,** and Dian saw her first gorilla. The moment made a lasting impression. Life for her would never be the same again.

After nearly seven weeks, Dian's vacation was almost over, but she had one last trip to make—a visit to the Forresters in Salisbury, Rhodesia. There she met Pookie's brother, Alexie. They liked each other at once and agreed to meet up in the United States.

Wildlife photographer Alan Root films an Egyptian goose nest.

In Fossey's words:

"Sound preceded sight. Odor preceded sound in the form of an overwhelming musky-barnyard humanlike scent…. Immediately I was struck by the physical magnificence of the huge jet-black bodies blended against the green palette wash of the thick forest foliage."

(Fossey describes her thoughts on seeing the gorillas for the first time, in *Gorillas in the Mist*)

Gorilla Country

This low-lying cloud is in the dense rainforest of the Virunga Mountains. Rwanda, "the land of a thousand hills," is a country of great natural beauty.

The parts of central Africa that Dian Fossey first saw in 1963 were thought by many to be too dangerous for tourists to visit. However, Dian was not scared off by danger, and the uncertainty only added to the excitement of her trip. Zaire, now known as the Democratic Republic of Congo, Rwanda, and Uganda had all recently become independent from white Western rule. Old **tribal conflicts,** such as that between the Tutsi and Hutu peoples in Rwanda, were stirring up violence. The new governments were struggling to keep control, and trouble could flare up suddenly and unexpectedly. In the same year as Dian's visit to Africa, a rebel army of Tutsi soldiers attempted to take over the government of Rwanda. They failed, and the Hutus took revenge with a large-scale **massacre** of Tutsi people. A few years later, Dian was to become caught up in a similar conflict in Zaire.

The terrain and climate of the Virunga volcanic region, along the borders of Rwanda, Zaire, and Uganda, could hardly have been more difficult for Dian. It is an area of steep mountains covered by a dense rainforest of hardwood trees and vines. The undergrowth is thick with huge-leaved nettles that can sting through several layers of clothing and razor-sharp thistles. In places, the vegetation is almost impossible to get through, particularly for someone as tall as Dian.

A head for heights

The gorillas that so fascinated Dian live at heights above 10,000 feet (3,000 meters), where the air is thin and it difficult to breathe. Mists and rains are almost constant, and regular storms produce hailstones big enough to dent a tin roof. At night, the temperature often drops well below freezing. Spending any length of time in the Virunga Mountains would have been difficult for a fit person. But for Dian, a heavy smoker with **asthma** and other health problems, it seemed very unwise. Her success, against all the odds, shows how determined she was.

In spite of these difficulties, central Africa has a particular fascination for **anthropologists** studying the origins of human life. As long ago as the 1870s, Charles Darwin, the great Victorian naturalist, suggested that human beings had originated in Africa. This was because our closest animal relatives, the chimpanzees and gorillas, were found there. For anthropologists, studying the surviving great apes became a means of learning about the origins of human beings.

*These national park guards are using a **panga knife** to cut through the dense vegetation of the Virungas region.*

This occupational therapist works with a child. The photograph was taken around the time Dian worked at Kosair Children's Hospital. It shows the kind of work Dian did with young polio victims there.

After her exciting travels in Africa, Dian Fossey reluctantly returned to Louisville, and to her job as an **occupational therapist.** She spent most of her spare time writing about her experiences of seeing the rare mountain gorilla and meeting the Leakeys, then trying to sell the articles and photos to newspapers and magazines. Dian received many rejection slips, but eventually she got a few articles accepted by the local paper. She was paid $100.

Dian's friend, Alexie Forrester, wrote to her, and a few months later flew to the United States, where he planned to study. He and Dian spent Thanksgiving in 1964 together at her home in Louisville. By this time, it was obvious that a serious relationship was developing. The following year, they were engaged.

The chance of a lifetime

Then Dr. Leakey arrived in Louisville on a lecture tour. Grabbing the newspaper articles she had written, Dian joined the crowds flocking to hear this world-famous scientist talk about his work. After the lecture, Dian pushed her way through all the people wanting to talk to Leakey. Would he remember her from their first meeting three years earlier? To Dian's amazement, he did—and even asked about her injured ankle! Leakey was impressed by Dian's continued interest in gorillas and suggested she should come to work for him. He wanted someone to carry out a **census,** or head count, of the gorillas, which by now were threatened with **extinction.** It was an opportunity that Dian could not afford to pass up.

Louis and Mary Leakey were famous for their study of the origins of humans.

Going back

Leakey persuaded the Wilkie Foundation to fund the project. Later on, when the project took off, funding would come from the National Geographic Society. Dian quit her job, against the advice of friends, family, and fiancé, and got ready to depart. She also had her appendix taken out—Leakey had told her she must before she could leave for Africa. This was, he said, because there were no hospitals nearby where she could have the operation if it was necessary later on. Dian went ahead and had it done— only to discover that it was not necessary at all, but was Leakey's final test of her determination! Finally, on Monday, December 19, 1966, Dian boarded the plane that would take her back to Africa.

The Study of Primates

Although she did not yet know it, Dian Fossey was to become one of the best-known twentieth-century **primatologists,** or people who study the group of mammals that includes monkeys, apes, and humans. It was Louis Leakey who most influenced and helped Dian in her study of gorillas. Their meeting at Leakey's **dig** in Tanzania in 1963 had encouraged her to go to the Virunga Mountains to watch gorillas. Now, three years later, Leakey had offered Dian the chance of a lifetime.

But Dian was not the first to do such work. In 1956–57, Leakey had sent two women to study gorillas—first Rosalie Osborn and then Jill Donisthorpe—but each lasted only a few months. Then, in 1959, a zoologist named George Schaller spent a year conducting pioneering research on great apes. In *The Year of the Gorilla,* Schaller described the family life of mountain gorillas. Schaller's book also taught Dian what to do if a male gorilla charges: do not run away, but sink to the ground and stay completely still so you do not appear threatening. It was Dian's job to continue Schaller's work. But no one realized that she would go on to do so much more, developing new techniques of close observation that would have a major impact on the study of **primates** and other animals in the wild.

George Schaller started the detailed study of gorillas in the Virungas. Later, Dian continued and extended his work.

Dian had also heard of an earlier primatologist named Carl Akeley. He had been a hunter and **taxidermist** until he realized how rare mountain gorillas were becoming. In 1925, he persuaded the king of Belgium, who ruled Rwanda at the time, to turn the Virunga Volcanoes into Africa's first national park so that gorillas would be protected from hunters and poachers.

The ape ladies

In the early 1960s, Leakey inspired another primatologist, Jane Goodall, to begin her important study of chimpanzees at Gombe Stream Reserve in Tanzania. Dian went to Gombe before starting her study of gorillas to learn about camp organization and data collection. She was at first in awe of Jane, but later became very friendly with her, and valued her "patience and sense of humor." Jane, Dian, and another researcher, Biruté Galdikas, who studied orangutans, were all recruited by Leakey. Together they became known as the ape ladies.

Jane Goodall worked with chimpanzees at Gombe Stream Reserve.

LOUIS LEAKEY

Leakey was born in Kenya in 1903, the son of English **missionaries.** Most of his childhood friends were black Africans of the local Kikuyu tribe. As a teenager, he became a member of the tribe, and later a tribal elder, or wise man. He went to England to study at Cambridge University, and there he met and married Mary, an **archaeologist.** Together, they investigated the ancient ancestors of humans on **digs** in Africa, Israel, and the United States. Louis Leakey died in October 1972.

Kabara Meadow

Here, Dian tracks gorillas. She quickly learned how to spot broken twigs, footprints, and dung, signs that showed where gorillas had been.

Louis Leakey met Dian when she arrived in Nairobi, Kenya, to begin her new job. There was a lot to organize. First she needed transportation. Dian chose an old Land Rover, and named it "Lily." Then they shopped for essential supplies and equipment. At last, in January 1967, Dian set out for Kabara Meadow, on the north side of the Virunga Mountains. Alan Root, the wildlife photographer she had met there on her previous visit, went with her.

Finding her feet

Root stayed with Dian for a few days to help her set up camp. When he left, Dian was overwhelmed by a sense of panic. Would she be able to cope on her own? Everyone had put such faith in her, but was she up to the task? The arrival a few days later of Sanwekwe, the experienced **tracker** Dian had met on her holiday three years earlier, calmed her fears. She quickly got down to work identifying and counting the gorillas.

At first, Dian's approaches to the gorillas were clumsy. She tried to get too close, too quickly. Either she disturbed them and they ran off, or she provoked them into screaming and charging her. Standing her ground, as she knew she must, was easier said than done. She could do so only by "clinging to surrounding vegetation for dear life."

In Fossey's words:

*"I learned to scratch and groom and beat my chest. I imitated my subjects' **vocalizations,** munched the foliage they ate, kept low to the ground and deliberate in movement—in short, showed that my curiosity about them matched theirs toward me."*

(From *National Geographic*, April 1981)

Disaster!

After six months, Dian seemed to be making progress at last. The gorillas became more tolerant of her as she started to imitate their noises and eating habits. But then disaster struck. The civil war in the Congo flared up again, and one day, without warning, a band of soldiers appeared at Kabara. They looted the camp and roughly forced Dian back down the mountain to the park headquarters, where they kept her prisoner.

This could have been the end of Dian's project. But, once again, her determination won out. She tricked her guards into going with her across the border to Uganda in Lily the Land Rover, by saying that she had money at a friend's house. But when they got there, she dashed into the house and refused to leave. The guards had to return without Dian, without money, and even without Lily the Land Rover!

Dian did not want to appear threatening to the gorillas, so she crouched low to the ground, kept still, and copied their behavior.

Karisoke

Porters carried equipment and supplies up to Karisoke.

Dian was lucky to escape from the Congo with her life. At first, it seemed certain that she would have to abandon her research. But as she looked back at the Virunga Mountains from a safe distance, she realized that there could be other alternatives. The Congo was closed to her. But the gorillas knew no national boundaries. If they lived on the Congo side of the mountains, it was possible that they would also be found on the Ugandan or Rwandan sides.

*"The [plateau] was... beautiful. The large umbrella shapes of the **Hagenia** trees gave a protective air to the camp. The swiftly flowing river added a touch of musical magic to complete the setting."*

(From Alan Goodall, *The Wandering Gorillas*)

While she decided what to do, Dian went to stay in Rwanda with Alyette de Munck, a Belgian woman who owned **plantations** there. A friend had assured Dian that there were no gorillas in Rwanda. But Dian disagreed. The old camp at Kabara Meadow lay only a few miles to the north of the border. A little to the east, but in Rwanda, lay the twin peaks of Mounts Karisimbi and Visoke. Between the two mountains was a level plateau, that Dian could just see through her binoculars. It looked like the ideal place to start again.

A new start

In September 1967, only two months after she had been kicked out of Kabara, Dian set out once more. She drove with Alyette to a village at the foot of the mountains. From there, she began a climb of several hours, accompanied by a long trail of barefoot porters who carried on their heads tents, food, and equipment for the difficult months ahead.

Despite the pouring rain, the site that Dian had spotted from a distance was everything she had hoped for, and more. She immediately fell in love with the beauty of the place, calling it "Karisoke," a combination of the names of the two mountains on either side of the plateau. As she lay in her tent that first night, Dian recognized the unmistakable pock, pock, pock sound of a gorilla beating its chest. They were there, in the forest, just as she had predicted!

This corrugated iron cabin at Karisoke was Dian's home for eighteen years. Cooking was usually done outside over a campfire.

*"Even on sunny days the slopes are difficult—slippery, wet, and tangled... It is almost impossible to walk anywhere without cutting a trail with a **machete**... Fields of nettles deliver a punishing sting that feels like electric needles even through two layers of clothing."*

(Sy Montgomery, in *Walking with the Great Apes*)

Dian's Discoveries

This is a male lowland gorilla. Gorillas are highly sociable animals that live in close family groups.

Gorillas are the largest of the great apes, the animal family to which human beings also belong. Part of what makes them so fascinating is their similarity to us—they are humans' closest relatives other than chimpanzees. But Dian discovered that gorillas are just as interested in us as we are in them. During her years of study, she developed a close relationship, almost a friendship, with several individuals. Often she would observe them watching her with curiosity and intelligence. Sometimes it was difficult to know who was studying whom. This was a far cry from the traditional view of gorillas as savage monsters.

Dian studied mountain gorillas, a group closely related to—but distinct from—the lowland gorillas found in other parts of Africa. The lowland variety are relatively common. This is the kind you are most likely to see in a zoo, although in the wild they are more cautious and shy than their mountain cousins. Surprisingly, mountain gorillas were unknown until 1903, when they were found by German hunter Oscar von Beringe. It is from von Beringe that they take their Latin name *Gorilla gorilla beringei*.

Gentle giants

Mountain gorillas are massive animals. Their arm span and their height can both be over six feet (two meters). Adult males are called silverbacks because of the silvery-gray color of the fur on their backs. Each family group is led by just one silverback. He is the dominant male and can weigh as much as two adult humans. Gorillas eat an almost solely vegetarian diet, including wild celery, berries, roots, bark, and bamboo sprouts. They have to spend about one-third of their day eating in order to stay healthy.

Gorillas had always been thought of as dangerous creatures. Explorers of the nineteenth century mistakenly depicted them as monsters. In 1933, the movie *King Kong* showed actress Fay Wray in the clutches of a vicious, ten-story-tall gorilla. Thanks to the observations of George Schaller and Dian Fossey, people eventually realized that gorillas are, if unprovoked, gentle, timid animals—and vegetarians!

Dian's research added greatly to our knowledge of these animals. She counted them, tracked them, photographed them, and tape-recorded their sounds. She even weighed and analyzed their dung to collect evidence of their diet and diseases. When they died, she carried out **post-mortem** examinations. This was the first time anyone had attempted such a detailed study of gorillas.

The silver-colored fur characteristic of an adult male gorilla develops by about fifteen years. Adult males often weigh twice as much as females.

Coco and Pucker

Dian Fossey was destined never to have a baby of her own. But she experienced some of the pains and joys of motherhood when two sick, orphaned baby gorillas came to Karisoke.

The first arrived in early 1969, near death from starvation and with infected wounds from the wire that had been used to tie it up. It was supposed to be going to a zoo in Cologne, Germany. Ten adult gorillas had died trying to protect the baby from poachers. To make matters worse, it was a park official who had organized the "kidnapping" and paid the poachers, when it was his job to protect the animals. He was in a panic because the gorilla was obviously very sick, and if it died, the zoo would not pay up. Despite all this, Dian agreed to try to nurse the gorilla back to health. She named it Coco.

A few days later, another infant in a similar condition was brought to the camp. This one was named Pucker, and was also intended for the German zoo. For the next two months, Dian stopped all her field work while she concentrated on getting "her babies" well again. She turned her cabin into a mini-forest, with branches and vines to make the baby gorillas feel at home. Staff were sent out to collect tasty gorilla food such as blackberries. The cook was even ordered to make special baby-gorilla meals, but he left in protest!

For two months, Dian nursed Coco and Pucker back to health.

Dian spent hours grooming their coats, combing through their fur with her fingers. This is a social activity that baby gorillas learn from their mothers.

Coco and Pucker were put in boxes and sent to a zoo in Germany in May 1969.

Saying goodbye

Dian's close involvement with the baby gorillas vastly increased her scientific knowledge and understanding of the animals she was studying. She watched them feeding at close range. She learned what their sounds meant to each other. She copied them and discovered that she could communicate with them. She truly was part of a gorilla family. Dian desperately wanted to release Coco and Pucker back into the wild when they recovered their health, but the park official threatened to capture more baby gorillas if she did that. She was forced to allow them to be packed away in boxes and sent off to the zoo. Both of them died nine years later, in 1978.

ONGOING IMPACT	Gorilla language

Learning and imitating the sounds and actions gorillas use to communicate with each other allowed Dian to get much closer to gorillas in the wild. Her method was continued by scientists after her death and has been used in countless similar situations.

Gorilla Watching

As Dian spent more time in the Virungas, she made rules to enable humans to get close to the gorillas safely. This was important, because many students and researchers came to Karisoke to work, and they needed guidance on what to do.

Dian sets up recording equipment. The hours of tapes and films provided evidence for her research.

1. Never run from a gorilla charge. Crouch low to the ground and don't look the gorilla directly in the eye. It will most likely stop and leave you alone.
2. Do not try to touch the gorillas. You can let them touch you but if you make the first approach, they may think you are being aggressive.
3. Always let a gorilla know you are close. Make a humming noise such as "*uum—aah—uum—aah.*"
4. Always move slowly near gorillas. They are easily startled.
5. Never go near gorillas when you are sick. It is possible to pass on human diseases against which gorillas have no defense.
6. Never stand in the way of a gorilla. This is their territory and they have the right of way.

Sticking to the rules

By following her own guidelines, Dian was accepted by the gorillas. She got to know them as individuals, giving them names such as Uncle Bert (after her own uncle) and Digit (because of his deformed finger). She even discovered that each gorilla has a unique noseprint, formed by the pattern of wrinkles above the nostrils.

Dian learned to identify each gorilla by the distinctive shape of its nose and the wrinkles above it.

To most people, some of the gorilla habits that Dian revealed seem disgusting or even cruel. For example, gorillas often make belching noises when they are content. They will even eat their own dung. Dian believed that this was a way for gorillas to absorb into their bodies certain vitamins that had already been partly digested on their way through the gut. It did not appear to do the animals any harm.

Another practice that seems dreadful to us is **infanticide,** or the deliberate killing of infants. If a mountain gorilla father dies young—for example, if he is killed by poachers—his females will join another group. The silverback in the new group will instinctively kill any unweaned babies with bites to the skull and thigh. Dian thought this happened so that the females would be ready to mate again sooner than if they had to wait two or three years for the infant to be weaned. The new silverback could then spend that time looking after his own, rather than someone else's, offspring.

INFANTICIDE

Infanticide accounted for the deaths of six out of 38 mountain gorilla infants born over a thirteen-year period, from 1967 to 1980. Victims died instantly as the result of one severe, crushing skull bite from an adult male gorilla.

Dian's War

Dian sent some of her trackers on antipoaching patrols. She encouraged them to destroy traps and capture poachers, but not injure them.

ONGOING IMPACT · Conservation

Dian Fossey felt passionately that her role was not just to observe, but to protect "her" gorillas. This approach, that she called "active conservation," is now commonly used throughout the world to protect other endangered animals.

The two main threats to mountain gorillas came from farmers and poachers. Dian encountered both almost from the moment she founded Karisoke. Two Tutsi herders with about 100 cattle wandered across the meadow as she pitched the tents. Only an hour or so later, two poachers from the Batwa, another local tribe, came to see her. They carried their bows, arrows, and spears, and actually offered to show her a gorilla family just 45 minutes away. Dian gave them a stern warning that she would not tolerate their activities.

Farmers

Dian would not have minded the cattle if there had been fewer of them. But for the Tutsi, cattle are a status symbol—a sign of importance—so they kept many more than they needed for their livelihood. The cattle crushed and spoiled the plants that gorillas eat, forcing the gorillas higher up the slopes where it was too cold and wet for them to survive. Dian was determined to protect the gorillas—at any cost. At one point, she even began shooting some of the cattle.

Poachers

The harm done by poachers was much more direct. Gorillas were a good source of income to them in several ways. Their hands could be cut off, made into bizarre ashtrays, and sold to tourists as souvenirs. Their skulls were sold to sportsmen as hunting trophies. Sometimes, a whole family was slaughtered to capture a baby that could be sold to a zoo. The poachers were not officially allowed to do any of this in the park, which was a **sanctuary.** But Dian suspected that they escaped arrest and punishment because the poorly paid park guards could be bribed to ignore their actions.

In Fossey's words

Dian's methods were seen by many as questionable:

"We stripped [the poacher] and spread-eagled him outside my cabin and lashed... him with nettle stalks and leaves.... That is called 'conservation'—not talk."

(Dian Fossey, quoted by Sy Montgomery in *Walking with the Great Apes*)

Taking control

Dian took the law into her own hands, destroying the traps, arresting poachers, and then handing them over to the police. She even let the superstitious Batwa believe she was a witch with supernatural powers so they would be terrified of her. All this horrified her friends. To them, Dian was an American abroad apparently interfering in ancient and established customs. The Rwandan authorities turned against her. It was the beginning of a war.

Dian's trackers destroyed this poacher's trap. Traps like this were difficult to spot in the undergrowth.

Camp Life

The camp cook baked bread in an outdoor oven.

FEEDING THE CAMP

The camp was in a national park, so no food could be grown there. There were a few hens that visitors sometimes brought as gifts. They became camp pets, and occasionally laid eggs. The head porter brought mail and supplies by motorbike from Ruhengeri, an hour's drive away twice a week. Some produce, like beans and potatoes, was bought from farmers around the park.

Camp staff at Karisoke included **trackers,** a cook, a woodsman, antipoaching patrols, a research assistant, up to three students at a time, and porters who delivered supplies and mail twice a week. The daily routine at Karisoke began around 5:30 A.M. for Dian, her students, and staff. Dian would tell everyone what their tasks were for the day—tracking, observing, counting for the **census,** or cutting away traps. Students often had research projects of their own to work on, and Dian encouraged them to do their research. But if any traps were found, the students were expected to cut them first, before getting on with their own work. For students with limited time in the field and tough deadlines, this rule was sometimes seen as being unfair. Even Dian admitted that she was a difficult person to work for.

A hard life

The evenings were spent writing up that day's field notes or studying gorilla bones—and doing the housework! Clothes were always wet and muddy, needing to be washed and hung out to dry. The mud seemed to be as thick on the floor of the corrugated metal cabins as it was outside, even though it was swept out every day. Karisoke was not a very sociable place, and there was nowhere to go to relieve the boredom. It was a hard life, and the students had very little contact with the outside world. Dian was totally dedicated to the gorillas, but most people lacked her commitment and could not stand it for long. Some left as soon as they could.

Passing friendships

Dian did manage to get along well with a few of Karisoke's longer-term visitors. One was Bob Campbell, a Scottish photographer based in Kenya. He spent nearly four years at Karisoke, on and off, photographing the gorillas for *National Geographic* magazine, and he became very close to Dian. Another friend was Ian Redmond, a student from England, whom Dian considered to be one of the finest researchers she knew. He became known affectionately as the "Worm Boy" because he had the rather smelly job of examining gorilla dung each day, looking for signs of worms that live in the digestive system.

Ian Redmond studied parasites and led antipoaching patrols at Karisoke.

Hazards and Health

The Rwandan region of the Virunga Volcanoes is not an easy place in which to live. It is isolated from towns and cities, from hospitals and doctors. It is often cold and wet, and it is home to many dangerous wild animals.

Anyone wanting to live there needed to be physically very fit just to survive. Yet Dian's health was never good. Perhaps it was no surprise to her that after fifteen years in the Virungas, she had a permanent, racking cough, and eventually needed extra supplies of oxygen to enable her to climb the steep path to Karisoke.

Buffalo can be extremely dangerous if approached incorrectly.

Dian speaks with a Tutsi tribesman and his cattle. To Dian, wandering cattle were a menace. But to the Tutsi, they represented wealth and status.

Dangerous times

Dian was never hurt by the gorillas. But one of her students was charged and rolled by a silverback, breaking several ribs, and then bitten badly in the neck. The student had taken a large group of people to see some gorillas he had been working with, to get them used to tourists. The gorilla had clearly seen the group of visitors as a threat and attacked. On another occasion, Sandy Harcourt, a student from England, was gored on the horns of a buffalo and nearly killed. Harcourt had charged at the buffalo, trying to drive it away, and the buffalo had simply charged back.

In Fossey's words:

*"I was... nipped by a sickly poacher's dog... and... I joked about it. But... everyone became most upset [because] **rabies** among wild dogs in Rwanda is sixty percent.... Rabies is... fatal without the series of injections."*

(From *Woman in the Mists*)

Going "bushy"

But possibly the worst problems were loneliness, isolation, and depression. People who spent months at a time at Karisoke talked of going "bushy," or forgetting how to live as a human being. Dian once said in a lecture she gave in New York that she could never remember to flush the toilet when she was back in town because she was not used to proper sanitation. Nevertheless, she added, she would not want to trade places and live in a city.

31

The "Big Degree"

Dian was good at her job and earned the respect of Dr. Leakey and other important scientists. But, as she herself often said, "You don't cut much ice in the scientific world without that Big Degree." She was referring to her own lack of university training in her field. Not only had she failed some of her **preveterinary** courses, but she had also never done any **postgraduate** work. This is a period of study that usually lasts several years, supervised by a university professor and leading to a **thesis,** a long piece of written work containing new information or original research.

It bothered Dian that she did not have an advanced university degree—and Leakey agreed that she should return to studying. With his help, Dian was accepted as a postgraduate student of animal behavior at Cambridge University. Dian was to begin her studies in England in January 1970.

For Dian, the beautiful surroundings of Cambridge were no substitute for the life she had grown to love in Africa.

Peanuts was the first gorilla to overcome his shyness, hold out his hand, and touch Dian.

The perfect present

Just before she left, Dian was out in the bush watching Peanuts, a young male gorilla. Dian and Peanuts started playing together, scratching and eating celery stalks. Then Dian lay back and spread her arms out. Peanuts came closer and actually touched her hand. Dian was so happy, she burst into tears! The photographer, Bob Campbell, captured the moment on film, and the photograph appeared in *National Geographic* magazine. It was "the best going-away present" Dian could have had.

Dr. Fossey

Dian spent several months each year in Cambridge for the next few years. She did not enjoy it, largely because it was all indoor work. She analyzed her data with computers, and used **sonographic** equipment to produce visual images of gorilla noises from her tape recordings. She longed for the great outdoors of Africa—but she stuck to her task. In May 1976, the Cambridge examiners agreed that her study of the mountain gorillas contained so much new information that she could be awarded a post-graduate degree, called a **doctorate.** She was Dr. Fossey at last! Dian returned to Africa as soon as she could that year.

In Fossey's words:

"Peanuts seemed to ponder accepting my hand. Finally he came a step closer and touched his fingers to mine. To the best of my knowledge this is the first time a wild gorilla has come so close to holding hands with a human being."

(From *Gorillas in the Mist*)

Digit

Digit was a very special gorilla for Dian. She first got to know him as a baby, when he was nothing more than a "playful little ball of disorganized black fluff" who would lie on his back, waving his stumpy legs in the air, inviting her to play. And she did, her scientific role completely forgotten. As Digit grew up, their special bond remained. Digit would often put an arm around Dian's shoulders, just like a human friend, and they would sit together for hours.

Tragic news

But in January 1978 Dian received the most terrible news. Ten-year-old Digit had been brutally murdered. As a young silverback, Digit had defended his family against poachers, sacrificing his life in the process. Ian Redmond and Nemeye, a **tracker,** found his mutilated body about two hours' walk from the camp. His belly and chest had been ripped open with spears. His head and hands had been hacked off to be sold as souvenirs.

"*[Digit's murder] unhinged her. She became dangerous to herself and to the Rwandans, because of her volcanic temper and her methods of interrogating alleged poachers.*"

(Mary Smith of *National Geographic* magazine, describing Fossey)

Dian had a very close relationship with Digit.

These workers are digging a new grave in the gorilla graveyard at Karisoke. Digit was buried closest to Dian's cabin.

Taking action

Dian was devastated. Digit's body was brought back to Karisoke and buried close to Dian's cabin. Dian and Ian Redmond talked about what to do next. At dawn, she sent Ian to check on the other members of Digit's group. Then she went into action. She offered a cash reward to anyone with information about Digit's killers, and sent pictures of his headless, handless corpse to every conservation pressure group and wildlife magazine in the world. This was the start of the Digit Fund, now the Dian Fossey Gorilla Fund.

Soon after Digit's death, Dian spotted a band of poachers on the fringe of the camp. She and her men caught one of them. They tied him up overnight and questioned him before handing him over to the police. To her horror, she learned that a local merchant had offered $20 for the head and hands of a silverback gorilla. So Digit had died for just a few dollars! Dian said afterwards that she came close to killing the man with her bare hands.

ONGOING IMPACT) **Digit Fund**

Dian was determined that Digit should not have died in vain. She used the Digit Fund to pay for antipoaching patrols to keep it from ever happening again. It also raised public awareness of the plight of gorillas and other endangered species.

35

Gorillas in the Mist

After Digit's death, nothing seemed to be going right for Fossey. Another of her favorite gorillas, Uncle Bert, was shot by poachers, along with a female and an infant in his group. Dian's own health was failing—she was now troubled by a constant, nagging pain in her hips and back. Because of Dian's temper and uncompromising views, relationships with almost everyone—the Rwandan authorities, her staff and the students, other conservation groups, and even her **sponsors** like the National Geographic Society and the Leakey Foundation—were poor. No one seemed to understand or support her point of view. People were starting to say that she could no longer run Karisoke.

In August 1979 a professor of **primatology** from Cornell University visited Karisoke. Dian told him of the pressure on her to leave, but said that she had nowhere to go. The professor offered her a temporary teaching post at Cornell, and with some reluctance, Dian took it. She did not want to leave the gorillas, but even she could see that she needed a break.

Dian spent three years at Cornell giving lectures on the great apes. She was a successful and sympathetic teacher.

Dian says goodbye on her way to take up her post at Cornell University.

Her teaching schedule was relatively light, leaving her enough time to finish writing her book, *Gorillas in the Mist,* about her experiences in the Virunga region. To relieve the agonizing pain in her back and hip, she underwent surgery. She made friends at the university. She was even paid a decent salary. It was really a very normal life—but it was not home. Dian would look at the photos of her gorillas and feel tremendous guilt, as if she had betrayed them by leaving.

In 1983, *Gorillas in the Mist* was published and became an immediate best seller. Dian was persuaded to do a promotional tour. She was eager to do anything to raise awareness of the plight of mountain gorillas, although meeting so many people and signing copies of her book was not her idea of fun. Warner Brothers and Universal Pictures snapped up the film rights. The film, starring Sigourney Weaver as Dian, was a box-office hit when it was finally released in 1987.

The actress Sigourney Weaver is still an active supporter of the Dian Fossey Gorilla Fund.

ONGOING IMPACT	The film

Dian never saw the film *Gorillas in the Mist,* but she knew it was being made. She must have realized that this world-wide publicity would make sure the gorillas—her gorillas—would never be forgotten.

Return to Karisoke

In Fossey's words:

"[Tuck] smelled my head and neck, then lay down beside me… and embraced me!… She did remember me!… I could have happily died right then and there and wished for nothing more on earth… because [she] had remembered."

(Fossey, quoted by Farley Mowat, in *Woman in the Mists*)

Karisoke did not fare well during Dian's three-year absence. Her antipoaching patrols were abandoned, and a number of gorillas were killed. Her **sponsors,** the National Geographic Society, began to feel that perhaps she should be invited to return and resume her work there. Dian enthusiastically packed her bags and booked her flight back to Africa. But her joy at the thought of going back was mixed with great anxiety. Would the gorillas—who were animals, after all, and not human—remember her?

A happy reunion

In July 1983, on her first day back at camp, Dian went out into the forest in search of her friends. She met a female gorilla named Tuck, whom she had known well. Tuck did exactly what humans do when they meet someone they have not seen for years—she stopped, stared, and then walked up to Dian. Checking that it was indeed her, Tuck gave her a warm hug. Other gorillas in the group came over and joined in. It turned into a big group hug, with everyone belching and grunting with contentment!

Gorillas were often fascinated by Dian's pencil and notebook. Sometimes they took them out of her hands.

Gorilla tourism

By now, Dian's main concern was no longer the scientific study of gorillas. They were her family, and their protection was all that mattered to her. Unfortunately, this led Dian into bitter conflict with the Rwandan authorities yet again, as her "war" against the farmers and poachers continued. Their presence in the area was bad enough, but Dian was also opposed to uncontrolled gorilla tourism. She objected strongly to the invasion of their habitat and privacy.

The Rwandan government wanted a substantial income from tourism, but Dian stood in their way. It was even suggested that Karisoke should be turned into a camp for tourists, with only a few scientists in residence, chosen by the government. Dian was horrified. It seemed that she had no friends left in Rwanda, only enemies.

Dian's tactics angered some Rwandan officials, but she became popular among Rwandan people, who realized that she had helped to put their country on the map. She also made Rwandans aware of the benefits of protecting gorillas in order to encourage tourism. For the tourists, a live gorilla would always be worth more than a dead one.

Dian and her guards stand beside a pile of confiscated poacher's snares.

Dian's Murder

An American student, Wayne McGuire, arrived at Karisoke in August 1985. He intended to do research on whether male silverbacks contributed to the care of their infants and if so, how this affected the infants' survival. He mostly got along well with Dian, though he was shocked at how ill and frail she looked.

But at around 6:00 on the morning of December 27, one of Dian's African staff members burst into his cabin shouting, *"Dian kufa!"*—"Dian is dead!" McGuire followed the man back to Dian's cabin, where he saw her dead body lying on the floor of her bedroom. She was 53 years old. A deep cut ran from her forehead, over her nose, and across one cheek. She had been hit with a **machete.** Her possessions had been thrown about and smashed, but nothing had been stolen—about $3,000 in cash, some jewelry, and expensive camera equipment lay untouched. She was buried beside her great gorilla friend, Digit, in the graveyard beside her cabin.

The investigation

McGuire took over running Karisoke while the police investigated the murder. Several Rwandans were arrested and questioned. All were released without charge. Then McGuire was tipped off that the police were going to arrest him for the murder. They believed that McGuire was jealous of Fossey's success and wanted to steal her research.

This is Wayne McGuire observing one of the gorillas at Karisoke.

Dian's final resting place is at Karisoke. Her grave, surrounded by stones, lies next to where Digit was buried.

McGuire was very frightened. He did not want to leave until he had finished his research, but he did not want to end his life in an African jail, either. He flew back to the United States in the summer of 1986. A Rwandan court tried McGuire in his absence and convicted him of the murder of Dian Fossey, but McGuire has always said he was innocent.

Without a proper trial, we may never know for certain who killed Dian. She had made many enemies. It could have been one of the poachers, or a farmer, or one of her enemies at the park or in the Rwandan government. It could even have been one of her staff who had a dispute with her. But no evidence has ever been found. The true identity of Dian's killer remains a mystery.

In McGuire's words:

"Dian considered herself the mother of the Karisoke gorillas: they were her family, more important to her than people, she told me. Protecting them is what she dedicated her life to, and what she died for."

(Wayne McGuire, quoted in *The Sunday Times*, April 1987)

Dian's Legacy

Dian has a typically close encounter with a young gorilla. But who was studying whom?

The Karisoke Research Center carried on without Dian. Today it is run by the Dian Fossey Gorilla Fund International, which she started as the Digit Fund in 1978 after Digit's death. Another conservation group, the Mountain Gorilla Project (MGP), was also set up. This trained guards to patrol the volcano park area to protect its wildlife, and developed controlled gorilla tourism and conservation education.

Protecting the habitat

Both Karisoke and the MGP have had a lasting impact on conservation in Rwanda. People there now realize what a valuable resource the animals are, especially rare ones such as the mountain gorilla. Schools run education programs teaching children to value the rain forest and its wildlife. Public attitudes against poaching have helped to reduce this practice. Even the farmers are beginning to think of ways of making a living without damaging the habitat for the gorillas. As a result, gorilla numbers have risen from 242 in 1981 to about 500 today.

Dian was unhappy about using the gorillas as a tourist attraction. But since her death, other researchers have felt it is the only way of ensuring their survival. Bill Weber, a member of the MGP, used Dian's methods of communicating with the gorillas to get some of them used to groups of tourists. Weber's plan has been very successful. Tourists paid an entrance fee to the park, and were then escorted to a point where they could watch the gorillas. Some of the money raised went to the park, and some to the Rwandan government. Tourism from gorilla watching became the largest source of foreign money after tea and coffee.

The years since Dian Fossey's death have seen more violent upheavals in Rwanda. Fighting between the Rwandan Patriotic Front and the government has broken out several times. The conflict at several points in the early 1990s was so serious that Karisoke had to close and all its staff members were **evacuated.** It reopened, but was forced to close again because of more fighting. Tourism only started up again in the late 1990s.

A lasting tribute

Dian Fossey's research has significantly changed our understanding of apes and their importance in the history of humans. But her life's work was much more about saving the mountain gorillas from **extinction.** Dian's determination has been an inspiration to other researchers, and her work continues today.

Others continue Dian's work, when peace allows. Tourists and researchers began returning to Karisoke in 1999.

Timeline

1932	Dian Fossey is born in Fairfax, California.
1938	Fossey's parents divorce.
1939	Fossey's mother marries Richard Price.
1948	Fossey leaves Lowell High School and enrolls at Marin Junior College in Kentfield, California, to study business.
1950	Enrolls at University of California as **preveterinary** medical student.
1952	Transfers to San Jose State College, California, to study **occupational therapy.**
1954	Graduates with bachelor's degree in occupational therapy.
1955	Appointed director of occupational therapy at Kosair Children's Hospital.
1963	First visits Africa. Meets Dr. Louis Leakey.
1965	Fossey and Alexie Forrester engaged.
1966	Returns to Africa.
1967	Sets up base in Kabara Meadow. Forced out of Kabara Meadow by soldiers. Arrives at Karisoke. Engagement to Forrester ends.
1968	Death of her father, George Fossey.
1969	Coco and Pucker, two wounded baby gorillas, arrive at Karisoke. Fossey nurses them back to health.
1970	Peanuts, one of the gorillas at Karisoke, touches Fossey's hand. Fossey goes to Cambridge University, returning to Africa between terms.
1972	Death of Louis Leakey.
1976	Fossey is awarded her **doctorate** at Cambridge. Returns to Africa.
1978	Digit, one of the gorillas she studied, is found brutally murdered. Fossey sets up the Digit Fund (now the Dian Fossey Gorilla Fund).
1980	Fossey leaves Karisoke to take up a temporary teaching post at Cornell University.
1983	Fossey's book, *Gorillas in the Mist,* is published. Return to Karisoke.
1985	Death of Dian Fossey at age 53.

1987	The film *Gorillas in the Mist* is released.
1990	Karisoke closed because of political conflict.
1993	Karisoke reopened, then **evacuated** again, and subsequently burned down.
1998	Karisoke rebuilt and research resumed.
1999	First tourists allowed back to watch gorillas in the Virungas.

More Books to Read

Fossey, Dian. *Gorillas in the Mist.* New York: Houghton Mifflin Co., 1988.

Freedman, Suzanne. *Dian Fossey: Befriending the Gorillas.* Austin, Tex.: Raintree Steck-Vaughn Publishers, 1997.

Matthews, Tom L. *Light Shining through the Mist: A Photobiography of Dian Fossey.* Washington, D.C.: National Geographic Society, 1998.

Glossary

anthropologist someone who studies the origins and development of human life

archaeologist someone who studies the past by examining the remains of ancient civilizations and cultures

asthma disease that causes breathing difficulties

census count of people or animals

conservationist person who works to preserve nature and wildlife

dig site where archaeologists have been digging for evidence of life, such as bones

doctorate highest type of university degree

economic depression time when business is doing badly and money is in short supply

epitaph words written in memory of someone who has died

evacuated removed from a place of danger to a place of safety

extinction complete dying out of a species

Hagenia common rainforest tree on African mountains, with thick trunks and long, low branches

infanticide killing of babies

machete broad, heavy knife with a long blade

massacre mass killing of many people or animals

missionary person sent to a region to encourage belief in a particular religion

occupational therapy course of activities that helps people recover from illnesses or injuries

panga **knife** heavy, long-bladed African knife, or a Swahili word for a machete

plantation estate for growing trees or plants such as coffee or cotton

pneumonia serious disease of the lungs

postgraduate advanced university studies done after earning a first degree

post-mortem investigation of a dead body to discover the cause of death

preveterinary first part of the studies to become a qualified veterinarian

primate one of a group of mammals that includes monkeys, apes, and humans

primatologist person who studies primates

rabies infectious disease of animals and humans, causing madness and death

sanctuary safe place

sonographic representing sounds as a diagram or graph

sponsor person or business that gives money to support a project

taxidermist someone who collects and mounts animal skins for display

thesis long written study of a subject

tracker someone who finds and follows animals by their tracks

tribal conflict dispute between native tribes of people

vocalization noise made by an animal with its "voice" to communicate with other animals

zoology scientific study of animals

Index